# Franklin D. Roosevelt

*A Biography of an American President*

# Table of Contents

# Introduction

*"I ask you to judge me by the enemies I have made"*
—*Franklin D. Roosevelt*

How do you measure the success of a man's life; especially when he is in a position of power? Is it how he faces the challenges that come his way? Is it how far he came despite the challenges or obstacles that tried to knock him down? Is it how much he achieved on his own? When it comes to evaluating the terms of a sitting president, there are a multitude of factors that come into play to form a coherent conclusion.

Some say that a good president is determined by how they deal with the challenges that are thrown onto them by what is going on in other parts of the world. While others consider the greatness to come from how much initiative they take to solve the problems of their country, in spite and despite the state of the rest of the world. No matter how you measure greatness, there are some presidents that check both boxes, so to speak, for evaluation. The 32nd President, Franklin Delano Roosevelt is, arguably, one of these presidents.

Not only did he have to deal with his own health issues, but he also had to navigate a crumbling economy and a Second World War, among a multitude of other lesser-known challenges.

This book will trace a genealogical line through the life, career, presidency, and death of the 32nd president. To begin, we will take a look into the early life and childhood of Franklin D. Roosevelt; this is, of course, to see what, if any, notable events in his past were influential in his leadership role as president.

Following his early life, we will then move to his early political career, and the steps taken that led him to earn the title of president of the United States. Following his early political career, there will be a select few chapters that are focused on the impressive, and quite long, presidential reign of FDR. To round out this book, we will touch on the death and legacy of this great man and what he has left behind for so many to follow in his footsteps. Interspaced between each of these chapters will be quotes once uttered by this president of the United States that have lasted over time as being influential to many individuals.

Essentially, through reading this book, you will encounter the life of a great man who, while being forced into different hardships, both personal and political, was able to earn the respect of his countrymen and women and guide them through some of the darkest years of the 20th century.

\* \* \*

*"Take a method and try it. If it fails, admit it frankly, and try another. But by all means, try something."*
*—Franklin D. Roosevelt*

# Chapter One: The Young Franklin D. Roosevelt

*"There are as many opinions as there are experts"*
*—Franklin D. Roosevelt*

## Early Childhood of Franklin D. Roosevelt

Franklin Delano Roosevelt was born to James and Sara Delano Roosevelt on the 20th of January 1882. It would not be necessarily incorrect to say that the Roosevelt family was a family of luxury for its time. In fact, the family spread its time evenly between a large, yet respectful, family estate on the Hudson River Valley of New York and resorts all over Europe. In the midst of their privilege, their family did suffer some challenges over the years. For example, the birth of Franklin D. Roosevelt proved to be a difficult one, one in which his mother was laboring for hours and in fact, almost passed away during the delivery. This near loss of their son perhaps led to a more than expected level of pampering from his mother; an example of which would be that his mother would bathe him, or at least be in the room while he bathed until he was almost 10 years old. This pampering, however, was not solely from his mother. Roosevelt spent much time with his father over the years, which allowed him to develop many skills that other children his age would not have learned whether these other children had grown up in privilege or not. An example of this is the fact that Roosevelt, allegedly, was able to ride a horse independently by the age of 4. This expertise with horses transferred over into the winter months as Franklin would sleigh ride with his father all over their estate.

In addition to cultivating strong relationships with his mother and father, Roosevelt also developed impressive and close relationships with the governesses that cared for him. In total, it is said that Roosevelt had eight governesses that spanned his years living with his parents. Many of them left a strong impression on him during this time, including encouraging him to be the playful and prank-playing child that he naturally was, in addition to helping him develop an enthusiasm for education and specifically American history.

As a young man and child Franklin D. Roosevelt was taught privately at his home estate, or at whatever European resort they were frequenting at the time until he was around the age of 14. It was in these early years of teenagerhood that Roosevelt attended the Groton Preparatory School in, of course, Groton, Massachusetts. Attending this school was not easy for Roosevelt as he had to live away from his parents and family. However, in the midst of this challenge, Roosevelt eventually excelled in his studies, developing close relationships with some of the students and faculty at the preparatory school.

While this shift in education came with a shift in his location, the philosophy and ideology which were being instilled in him were the same. He was being taught to be a gentleman. Other lessons that were ingrained into this young man were those about the honor in assuming responsibility and helping those who were less fortunate than he, in addition to the many Christian values. Moreover, Roosevelt was taught that it is through helping others, and through public service, that he was meant to exercise these values.

All of this is to say that while the Roosevelts, Franklin included, lived a life of luxury, they were aware of their privilege and worked to help those who were less fortunate and who did not live in the same level of luxury as they did.

Allegedly, on a trip to Washington in 1887, Franklin D. Roosevelt, accompanied by his father, James, visited the White House just to say a quick "hello" to James' friend and comrade, the then President Grover Cleveland. It is said that Cleveland, after meeting Franklin, said that he wished someday for him to become the president of the United States. The rest, of course, fell into place quite soon after.

## Higher Levels of Education

It was in 1900 that Franklin D Roosevelt began his attendance at Harvard University. While he was talented and skilled in different areas of academics, it has been noted that during his time at Harvard, Roosevelt opted to spend the majority of his time on extracurricular activities and cultivating an impeccable social life. One aspect that did come out of the education and academic life of Roosevelt while attending Harvard University was his incredible respect for his fifth cousin, President Theodore Roosevelt. The legacy his cousin left was that of a champion who encouraged and advocated a larger role of the government in the economy of the United States. This was an impressive feat that stuck with Franklin for the remainder of his life, as such, influencing his political agenda once he entered into the political arena.

It was also during this time at Harvard University where Franklin D. Roosevelt met his would-be wife: Eleanor Roosevelt. It is important to note that Roosevelt was also the maiden name and soon-to-be-married name of Eleanor as she was Theodore Roosevelt's niece. This meant that Franklin and Eleanor were distant cousins of each other. Some controversial historians have alluded to the fact that if Franklin had not such high regard for his fifth cousin, he would not have fallen so hard for his niece. No matter, the relationship that developed between Franklin D Roosevelt and Eleanor Roosevelt would become a monumental and incredibly important relationship in both Roosevelt's personal life and in his political agenda. It was in 1905, early Spring to be specific, that the couple became engaged and married. This was also the year that Roosevelt attended his final year at Harvard University.

Following this final year, and his marriage to Eleanor Roosevelt, FDR began his attendance at the Columbia University Law School. While attending the school in order to become a lawyer and work in the political field, Roosevelt did not have much interest or enthusiasm for his studies. Despite this lack of enthusiasm, Roosevelt did indeed pass the bar exam only a few years later and began to work as a low-level clerk at the Wall Street firm in New York of Carter, Ledyard, & Milburn. While developing an impressive reputation for his hard work, Franklin D Roosevelt developed a type of neutral and indifferent opinion towards his career in the legal sector.

As a result, he turned his focus from law to politics, essentially actualizing the prediction made by Grover Cleveland many years earlier.

\* \* \*

*"Democracy cannot succeed unless those who express their choice are prepared to choose wisely. The real safeguard of democracy, therefore, is education." —Franklin D. Roosevelt*

# Chapter Two: Early Political Career

*"Let us never forget that [the] government is ourselves and not an alien power over us. The ultimate rulers of our democracy are not a President and senators and congressmen and government officials. But The voters of this country."*
—*Franklin D. Roosevelt*

### Gaining the Senate Seat

It was no secret to those around him that Franklin Roosevelt was no fan of practicing law. Rather, he'd made it clear to a few close acquaintances that he wanted to enter into the political arena. This goal and dream of holding a political office was of course influenced and encouraged by Franklin's admiration for his distant cousin, Theodore Roosevelt, in addition to Franklin's own dream of cleaning up the American government and politics in general. Even in the early 1900s, Theodore Roosevelt's tenure as president was still in the minds of many American citizens. As such, Theodore Roosevelt was still seen as a political powerhouse in the United States government.

As a result of being linked to Theodore Roosevelt, Franklin Roosevelt was seen to have natural political prowess. Furthermore, due to the fact that he came from a wealthier family, it was assumed that he would be able to pay for any political campaign himself without straining the monetary and financial resources of any political party. Therefore, piggybacking on his father's registered Democrat status, Franklin Roosevelt was accepted easily into the Democratic Party of the United States.

His first political race was for a seat in Congress for the legislative branch of the United States government. However, when the current holder of this position did not step down as it was assumed he would, Franklin did not get discouraged. Rather, he changed his political path and sought out a seat in the Senate, specifically the Senate seat from Dutchess County in Upstate New York. In 1910, Franklin D Roosevelt won the Senate seat with an overwhelming majority of the votes. This almost unanimous victory was largely thanks in part to the support of Franklin Roosevelt's cousin, Theodore. Although Theodore Roosevelt had always been known to be a Republican, he quietly yet fully gave his support to his cousin. It was this incredible victory of the Senate seat that had the American government predicting that Franklin Roosevelt entering politics was the second coming of the Roosevelt administration.

It was during his tenure in the United States Senate that Roosevelt began to dip his feet and have a hand in many different bills and committees. In 1912, Roosevelt rather vocally supported Woodrow Wilson as a Democratic nominee for the presidential election that year. This vocal and unwavering support for his fellow democrat brought tension to the Roosevelt family as a whole. This is because Theodore Roosevelt was also running for president in the selection as a third-party candidate. Of course, while many members of the Roosevelt family reprimanded and were disgusted by Franklin's image of abandonment towards his cousin, Theodore Roosevelt understood Franklin's political backing. Of course, Theodore Roosevelt did not win the election against Woodrow Wilson. Nor did the Republican candidate William Howard Taft.

Still holding his seat and position as a New York state senator during the Wilson administration, Franklin Roosevelt served on a number of different committees, including the House Committee on Agriculture and those concerned with the welfare of women and children in the United States. It was on these different committees that Franklin Delano Roosevelt learned the different ways in which government has influence over the American people

### Military Title

Due to Franklin D Roosevelt's strong support of Woodrow Wilson both in smaller political arenas and in his campaign to become president of the United States, Wilson brought the promotion and position of Assistant Secretary of the Navy to

Franklin Roosevelt's doorstep. Subsequently, as the First World War erupted, Woodrow Wilson kept Franklin in this position, close by his side as a close ally in the United States government. While in the role of assistant secretary, Franklin was largely in charge of overseeing the Navy civilian employees. As a result, he worked rather closely with different labor unions and union leaders.

Over his years in the role, Roosevelt was praised for how he dealt with different challenges and disputes. It has been noted that no strike occurred during his over seven years of holding the office of Assistant Secretary of the Navy. Roosevelt was considered to be a fair leader and mediator as he would take the interests and livelihoods of all parties into consideration and try not to let either party leave the dispute with nothing gained and everything lost.

Unfortunately, however, in 1914, Roosevelt ran for the Senate seat of a Republican of New York who was said to be retiring. However, due to the fact that Wilson needed a Republican in that seat for political reasons, Roosevelt was defeated in this Senate race. Of course, the loss of this Senate race was not entirely in vain and without purpose. Rather, it showed Roosevelt the importance of having the backing of the White House and other influential governmental groups when it comes to any political race. His family name, his family money, and his personal charisma and political aspirations alone would not be enough if he wanted to continue to climb the ranks of political office in the United States.

What's more is that in his role as Assistant Secretary of the Navy under the Wilson administration, Roosevelt developed many different politically inclined skills. These included: understanding of how the labor force worked; mediating disputes between different unions; different ways of managing government committees at different ranks and levels of government; logistical thinking and strategy surrounding war efforts. While he did not necessarily agree with many, if any, decisions made by President Woodrow Wilson in the First World War, Roosevelt did develop his own steady and focused opinions of how the United States should enter into, and conduct themselves in a war if a war was at hand.

In 1918, while still holding the position of Assistant Secretary of the Navy, upon developing these higher political skills and opinions, Franklin Delano Roosevelt began his next run for political office. This time, it would be for much more than a seat in Senate or as assistant secretary. This time it would be for the presidential office.

While it took many decades between the time Roosevelt first entered into the political arena and world of the United States Government and the White House, it was within this time where the future president developed many of the skills and the reputation that allowed him to be unanimously voted into the office of the president four times, and terms, in a row.

In fact, it was within his seat in the Senate, and his experience as Assistant Secretary of the Navy where Roosevelt learned the importance of connecting with the individual citizens of the United States while holding a political position in office. He learned that being a successful political figure meant that you did not only have the support of the population but the support of other political groups including the White House during your campaign.

As a result, Roosevelt developed and gained irreplaceable political experience during his years as a lower-level political and military figure. In turn preparing him for the role of the president of the United States, this primary experience in the political arena allowed Roosevelt to develop such a strong political agenda that helped him win both the popular and general elections for the presidential office.

* * *

*"If civilization is to survive, we must cultivate the science of human relationships- the ability of all peoples, of all kinds, to live together, in the same world at peace." —Franklin D. Roosevelt*

# Chapter Three: The Road to Becoming the President

*"The only thing we have to fear is fear itself."*
*—Franklin D. Roosevelt*

In a similar form to many of the presidents that came before him, and mirroring many of the presidents that were to follow, once Franklin D. Roosevelt entered into the political arena, the title of president was not far away.

When the Wilson administration was set to come to a close in the early 1920s, Roosevelt began to look for a fellow Democrat to run for the presidential office with him. For a few years during the First World War, Democrat Herbert Hoover was allegedly supposed to be the presidential running mate to Roosevelt, filling the vice-presidential candidacy on the Democratic ticket. However, Hoover rather suddenly declared himself to be a Republican rather than a Democrat, thereby leaving Roosevelt with no presidential running mate. That is until Governor James M. Cox stood up and took the title of the presidential nominee for the Democratic Party.

This was the last political move made by Franklin D Roosevelt before he became the nominee, the president-elect, and eventually the president of the United States; that is, Franklin D. Roosevelt won the nomination to be vice president on the presidential ticket with James M. Cox, in 1920. Even though Roosevelt and Cox campaigned strongly and impressively for the Democratic party, they lost rather dramatically to the Republican party as Warren G. Harding took office alongside president-elect Calvin Coolidge. As such, Roosevelt took time away from mainstream politics to become the vice president of the Fidelity and Deposit Company of Maryland in addition to other minor ventures in other areas of business.

It was during this time of pause in his political endeavors that Roosevelt vacationed in Campobello Island in New Brunswick, Canada, in 1921. It was here where he first contracted poliomyelitis. The symptoms of polio that Roosevelt suffered from were those that most individuals suffering from polio would also receive; namely a sore throat, fever, stomach pain, and other flu-like symptoms. Usually, the symptoms of polio last up to five days and are recovered from on their own. However, there are a small number of individuals who, after suffering from poliovirus, will exhibit and develop further and more serious symptoms that can last a lifetime. Unluckily for Franklin D. Roosevelt, he was part of this small percentage. While he generally recovered well from the virus, Roosevelt fought to keep the ability to walk and overall movement in his legs. It began with simply feeling pins and needles in his legs which required him to use an arm of a comrade or cane in order to stand or walk. However, over time, the paresthesia developed into full paralysis leading to Roosevelt requiring a wheelchair.

It has been suggested that such complications from contracting polio were due to the fact that Roosevelt suffered from an intense bout of influenza only a few years before his exposure to polio. In the late fall and winter months of 1918, Roosevelt boarded a USS Leviathan for a voyage during the First World War. Upon this voyage, there was a pandemic of severe influenza that killed the majority of crew and passengers on the ship. Some medical professionals believe the severity of the influenza, which Roosevelt survived, left his immune system compromised and crippled, therefore, giving way to the possibility of suffering such disastrous and extreme complications of the poliovirus, which he contracted just over two years later.

Interestingly, and to the credit of Franklin D. Roosevelt, suffering from polio and the lasting effects of the virus did not discourage Roosevelt from his lofty political goals and aspirations; he still had the dream and image of him cleaning up and generally improving the government of the United States. In fact, his health complications spurred him on as he pushed past and essentially ignored the request and urgency from his mother and wife to retire from politics. After abandoning the hope that he would once again walk, Roosevelt reapplied this hope and determination to his political career.

After he recovered from polio, or at least recovered to the best of his ability, he began once more to make a name for himself within the Democratic Party of the United States. In the mid-1920s, he enthusiastically and quite dramatically nominated Alfred E. Smith for president of the United States and would nominate Smith once more in 1928 for the same role and position. In return, and with thanks and gratitude, Smith would urgently suggest Roosevelt run for governor of New York; a role that Smith held for himself before becoming the Democratic nominee for president. It was during this run as governor of New York, Roosevelt was able to demonstrate and prove that his illness and negative experience with polio did not negatively affect his ability to be a political heavyweight. Instead, the campaign to become the governor of New York allowed Roosevelt to present himself as resilient, vital, and still in touch with the American people. Moreover, it allowed Roosevelt to become relatable to the people of the United States; after all who is more relatable to lead the country than someone who, while coming from luxury and money, has worked through his own set of hardships and still wants to help the unfortunate. Eventually, Roosevelt won the title of governor of New York even though the presidential election was won by Republican Herbert Hoover in 1928.

In an attempt to develop and cultivate his own political identity, much to the hurt feelings of Smith, Franklin Roosevelt did not look to his predecessor in the governor position for guidance. As a result, the platonic relationship that was once held between these two men slowly dissolved.

Part of this political identity was to show the American people, specifically the state of New York, his political agenda and how he was aiming and hoping to help them through what was turning out to be a difficult and extreme time for the United States economy. Specifically, Roosevelt as governor focused on relieving the tax burden of the common farmer and attempted to make utilities that were usually consumed publicly less expensive. As many of his programs to achieve this goal were favored by the New York population, Roosevelt was re-elected in his role as governor in 1930. However, as the depression that spanned the United States worsened and got much more severe, Roosevelt in turn and as a reaction became more driven in his political agenda. As such, he implored the state government to provide relief and aid to the state as a part of an economic recovery plan. Moreover, in 1931, he persuaded the heavily Republican-dominated government of the United States to create and establish a temporary emergency relief fund and administration to help families during this economic crisis. His aggressive and unrelenting political methods and how he dealt with the depression and economic crisis during this time is what helped boost Roosevelt's reputation in the Democratic party and eventually led to the Democratic presidential nomination in 1932.

It is significant to note that Franklin Roosevelt had contracted polio before he was even given the nomination for president of the United States as it goes to show how highly revered and thought of he was within the Democratic Party. Of course, winning the Democratic nomination was not easy, nor did it happen because individuals felt sorry for the man who was suffering from the rare complications of an illness. Rather, he used his illness to inspire a stronger political platform and to show that it was the mind of the presidential candidate that mattered more than his physical ability. Roosevelt proved that he was a strong contender for the American people and wanted to improve their quality of life after the First World War and in the midst of total economic collapse.

In fact, the illness and health of Franklin Roosevelt did not come into question, nor did it arguably affect his presidential leadership skills until the very end of his life and the very beginning of his fourth term.

\* \* \*

*"In politics, nothing happens by accident. If it happens, you can bet it was planned that way." —Franklin D. Roosevelt*

# Chapter Four: Key Moments of Roosevelt's Presidency

*"We have always held [on] to the hope, the belief, the conviction that there is a better life, a better world, beyond the horizon." —Franklin D. Roosevelt*

With having four terms as president, there are many key and memorable moments that have played a role in making Franklin D. Roosevelt one of the most memorable, revered, and respected presidents of the United States. For the simple reasons of organization and simplicity, we have chosen to divide and summarize these monumental and key moments into each of the four presidential terms.

## Roosevelt's First Term

### ❖ The First Election

After the Wall Street crash in 1929, the state of the United States economy was at the worst it had ever been since its establishment. It was assumed by many, both the laymen of America and by political figures, that it was the actions of past Republican presidents that had led to such an extreme economic crash. Therefore, if there was any silver lining to come from the Great Depression it was that the Democratic Party felt that this was their chance to take back, as it were, the role and title of President of the United States. In fact, the Democratic Party had yet to see a Democratic president at the head of the country since Woodrow Wilson whose tenure as president ended in 1921.

After much deliberation, the Democratic party chose Franklin Delano Roosevelt to represent them in the presidential election to face the Republican nominee, Herbert Hoover. Roosevelt won this presidential election and was inaugurated on the 4th of March 1933. However, what is perhaps lesser known is how much and how significant Roosevelt's victory was. Specifically, he won 472 out of the total 531 electoral votes in the United States; moreover, he won 57.4% of the popular vote. This result is significant as it was the first time a Democratic nominee won both the general election and the popular vote since the times of the Civil War.

Therefore, this result of the presidential election did not only place them in the presidential role, but it was also symbolic of how much faith and confidence the American public had in their new president-elect to help guide them through the economic crisis that was the Great Depression.

### ❖ The First Hundred Days

Of course, while Roosevelt had the confidence of the majority of the country, that did not mean that his presidency was made any easier. The condition of the United States when Roosevelt took office was, to put it quite simply, bad. A total of one whole quarter of the population of the United States was out of work or found themselves unemployed. Additionally, there were two million United States citizens who found themselves homeless. 32 of the 48 states in the 1930s had closed their banks. This led to an extreme number of individuals withdrawing their money from the bank and closing their accounts. This panic was due to the fact that the American public was afraid that they would not be able to retrieve their money at a later date. Moreover, they had lost trust in the banking institution and did not want their funds to be lost due to the closure of the banks. This panicked disillusionment about what happened with their money is due to the fact that the basic American citizens did not fully understand what was happening with their country and their money.

Being handed the country in such poor condition, Roosevelt got to work right away. Within his first few days of being elected president of the United States, Franklin Delano Roosevelt pulled the US Congress into a three-month-long session. This session of Congress, which spanned about 100 days in length, was designed for Roosevelt to push through as many bills as possible in order to rectify and recover from the economic downfall that had beheld his country. By the end of these 100 days, Roosevelt had pushed through 76 laws that were each meant to relieve the American people of the negative consequences and burden of the Great Depression, in addition to helping the United States of America as a country to recover from such economic downfall.

These first 100 days ended on June 11th, 1933. Just over a month after, on the 24th of July 1933, President Roosevelt took to the radio himself to address the American public. It is within this radio address that he spoke about the state of the country, the plan that had been pushed through to help the country recover from the past few years of suffering, and how the United States government was planning on ensuring the future of the United States, so as to not allow such an economic fall to happen again.

These first 100 days of the Roosevelt presidency have proven to be significant in more than one way. Of course, you must consider all of the bills that came out of these first 100 days, the New Deal being one of them which will be discussed later on in this chapter. However, what is perhaps the most significant of these first 100 days is the precedent that it set for many of the other presidents who followed him in the role. First, it was one of the very few times where the president took to a public forum of communication to address the American population. Furthermore, it lessened the gap between the American public and the United States government. The individuals and citizens of America felt as though the government actually cared about them and weren't simply looking for ways to help the banking system.

It was also in this first hundred days' radio address that the phrase "the first hundred days" was coined and the phenomenon that followed began. As a trend for most of the presidents that followed Roosevelt's four terms, the first hundred days of the presidency were looked at under a microscope. As such productivity had been accomplished within such a relatively short period of time, the first term of the Roosevelt presidency was one that many other presidents attempted to emulate in the hopes of being as productive throughout the rest of their presidential careers.

### ❖ The New Deal

One of the larger items, and most significant items, to come out of the first three-month-long session of the United States Congress, is of course the well-known New Deal.

Within the first hundred days of his presidency, and even within his presidential campaign and his inaugural address, Roosevelt made sure he explicitly mentioned and named who he blamed for the economic downfall of the United States. Specifically, he blamed the banks and the banking system.

Roosevelt claimed that the banks were more interested in building interest, gaining a profit, and the self-serving system of capitalism that held up the United States economy; In other words, Roosevelt blamed the banks, saying that they were more interested in using the American people's money to make money for themselves rather than to serve the American people and to keep the American people's money safe. After such a claim had been made, extreme and drastic moves were called on to rectify the situation. Specifically, this occurred in the form of what is now known as the New Deal.

The New Deal was a series of programs, financial reforms and regulations, and public work projects that were meant to be established and instilled into the United States population systematically so as to help regain focus, recapture the American spirit, and allow for recovery. Through the series of these programs, a three-fold method or philosophy for the recovery of the United States from the Great Depression was pulled. Namely, Roosevelt's plan aimed to relieve, recover, and reform. First, the New Deal aimed to relieve the individual American of the trials and tribulations, in other words, the negative consequences in general, of the Great Depression. The specific approach towards relief included programs aimed at the youth of America, the farmers, the unemployed, the elderly, and the disabled, in order to help them specifically recover from their monetary losses due to the depression. Secondly, Roosevelt aimed his plan at the recovery of the United States. His recovery was not only a recovery from past events, but it was to ensure the future of the country as well. As he was looking towards the future and not necessarily simply try to fix the problem at hand, Roosevelt made sure to include programs that could be sustained and implemented for many years to come. The president was also sure to include systems and programs that could be easily implemented and taken up once more if there were threats of such an economic disaster in the future. Lastly, the New Deal aimed to reform the United States of America, specifically, the banking system. Roosevelt aimed to fix and change the banking system, to ensure that such economic devastation would never happen again, or at least not to this extent.

There were two different phases of the new deal that were released during the first term of Franklin Delano Roosevelt's presidency. Within these two phases, many substantial and prominent groups and programs were set into place.

### The Federal Emergency Relief Administration

The main goal of the Roosevelt administration was to generally increase employment in the United States. As a result, the Federal Emergency Relief Administration started in 1933. Its full intention, or perhaps its most pertinent goal, was to address the needs of the poor population of the country. About 500 million dollars were spent on soup kitchens, blankets, nursery schools, and other amenities that helped encourage the poor population to gain employment. Two years later, however, the Federal Emergency Relief Administration was shut down and replaced with two subsequent agencies and programs, namely the Works Progress Administration, and the Social Security Administration. While the work of FERA was making headway, their goal proved to be too large for one Administration to tackle on its own, thus justifying the creation of two subsequent programs.

## Civilization Conservation Corps

In March of 1933, Roosevelt put into motion the systematic employment of unemployed men in different conservation projects that were needed around the United States during the summer months. By June of the same year, it was proposed that nearly a quarter of a million men were to be employed in emergency conservation work all over the nation. The Civilization Conservation Corps, otherwise known as the CCC, encouraged unemployed men to work on four different conservation projects such as planting trees and fighting forest fires for six months of the year. In the end, the CCC employed over 2 million unemployed men during the time of the national unemployment crisis.

## Agricultural Adjustment Administration

In May of 1933, the Agricultural Adjustment Administration, also known as AAA, was created by the Roosevelt administration. This Administration allowed for the increase of prices of crops grown all over the United States and helped reduce the stress of farm production by setting quotas and annual amounts for the farmers to reach. This act also gave modernized and innovative tools to the different farming communities across the United States, to help better increase the general production of their chosen crop.

In some very rare but still important cases, the AAA helped certain farmers and farming communities pay off mortgages or debts they had to their banks and government, in addition to creating payback contracts to allow for easier debt repayment.

## National Industry Recovery Act

On the 16th of June 1933, the National Industry Recovery Act, or a NIRA, was created. As the name would suggest, this act was put in place to help the industrial side of the United States recover from the deflation brought on by the Great Depression.

It should be noted that while this act was passed less than a week after the 100-day-long session of the United States Congress, it is still considered to be one of the more influential and significant acts to emerge from the first 100 days of Roosevelt's presidency.

There were two sections of this act that made it successful in reversing and recovering from the Great Depression. Specifically, the first section, the Public Works Administration, was set to use funds supplied by the government to help improve and rebuild much of the infrastructure around the United States. As a consequence, this created many jobs for the unemployed population. The second section of this act, known as the National Recovery Administration, focused on increasing the wages of those individuals who were employed. Generally, the philosophy behind these two sections of the larger National Industry Recovery Act, was that if the population of Americans were paid more, then they would spend more, giving money back to the United States economy.

## Second Term

The 1936 election proved to be one that was worrisome for Franklin Delano Roosevelt. This was because there were other notable Democrats within his party that had shown and proven their ability and interest in the presidential office. However, thanks in part to the second wave of his New Deal plan, in addition to the unfortunate death of Huey Long, the other nominee for the Democratic party and the one favored to be able to, over anyone else, beat out Roosevelt for the Democratic nomination for president, Roosevelt was elected once again, as not only the Democratic party's nominee for president but president of the United States as well. Rather than winning in a landslide as he did in the previous selection, he simply won two-thirds of the electoral votes. While his first term as president focused largely on recovering the United States from the Great Depression, his second term, if you could put a theme to it, would be foreign policy. Hitler and the Germans were gaining power over Europe, but the American people elected a president who would be able to combat Hitler's efforts and even lead them in war if it came to it.

Unfortunately for Roosevelt, his second term is considered to be one of his least productive or successful terms as president. It would seem as though Roosevelt fell to what is now known as "the second-term curse." Many presidents struggle with maintaining productivity and effectiveness in the role of president in their second term, in comparison to their first. This is perhaps due to the fact that such precedent and importance is placed on the first 100 days of the presidency. As such, some presidents, Roosevelt included, seem to lose their momentum.

That being said, Roosevelt did achieve and accomplish some significant acts as president in his second term. Primarily these were the Good Neighbor policy and trade agreements. In the presidential terms that came before Roosevelt, those holding the title of president withdrew the United States from many smaller wars and conflicts from around the world. For example, Americans were removed from Haiti, Cuba, and Panama. However, in 1933, Roosevelt signed into action an agreement that announced the right to decline or enter into any global conflict at their own discretion.

As a consequence of the signed contract, Roosevelt did not feel necessarily inclined to enter into the Second World War. However, as the years went on and his second term came to a close, Roosevelt entered into the war at least a little bit. He appointed a secretary of war and a secretary of the Navy to help keep track of the happenings overseas in addition to agreeing to send aid to the allied countries. Essentially, Roosevelt did all but enter America into the war officially.

However, in the next few years that would all change.

### Third and Fourth Terms

When it came time to the Democratic National Convention of 1940, there was some speculation as to whether or not Franklin Delano Roosevelt would try to run again for the presidential title. Of course, running a third time was extremely unprecedented as it was expected for each president to step down after two terms of four years each.

Unable to legally or constitutionally deny him the opportunity of running for a third time, the Democratic party decided that they would include Roosevelt in their list of nominees for president and to see what would happen. Essentially, if Roosevelt were to win, then he would be the presidential nominee for the Democratic party; yet, if Roosevelt were to lose then, the two-term expectation would be repeated once more and there would be no harm or foul to the electoral process or tradition. In the end, as history has shown, Roosevelt beat out all other Democratic challengers and nominees, making him the Democratic nominee.

The presidential election followed much in the same way as the Democratic election had. Many were unsure if they wanted to break the tradition of having only two-term presidents yet were conflicted by still considering Roosevelt a strong and respectable leader. This was also one of the rare times where a president, who had already served two full terms as president, was running for a third.

One of the largest worries of the American people, at the time, would be that they would be dragged and forced into another world war. Since the First World War, which had finished only a few decades earlier, had resulted in such an economic downfall, the American population was worried that the same thing would happen again. As a result, Roosevelt campaigned on a platform promising that he would not bring the

United States into the war happening overseas. This promise, in addition to his already overwhelming popularity and positive reputation, won Franklin D. Roosevelt the 1940 election, winning against both the popular vote and the electoral vote.

Of course, the third, and subsequently, the fourth term of Roosevelt's presidency, proved to be just as complicated as his first two. As tensions mounted in Europe and parts of Asia, Roosevelt met with Winston Churchill to talk about the impact of the war on Europe and how the American public could help aid Europe and the other allied countries. Believing that the United States Congress, based on the opinion and voices of the American people, would not allow for the United States to officially enter into the war, Roosevelt stood strong in his position to stay out of the conflict. Instead, he resolved to continue supplying aid to allied countries.

**Pearl Harbor**

As Japan began its own assault on the Republic of China, other parts of Asia, and other French-ruled countries, the Americans made their presence more widely known in these battles. It was in the early 1940s when Japan turned their attention to the United States.

On the morning of December 7th, 1941, the Japanese surprised the United States with an attack on the United States

Naval Base at Pearl Harbor in Hawaii. In total, the assault killed over two thousand American army men and civilians. There are many theories as to why Japan chose to attack the United States, and specifically the base at Pearl Harbor. One of these conspiracies includes the idea that Japan, witnessing the United States' growing influence in the war, was worried about what would happen if they actually entered into the war officially. Another reason would be as a retaliatory strike from the First World War.

No matter the reason for the attack on Pearl Harbor, it changed the direction for the Americans in the Second World War. Roosevelt, through some hesitation, officially entered the United States into the Second World War; first with a retaliatory attack on Japan. Fearing the results of the First World War and his predecessor Woodrow Wilson, Roosevelt took the opposite approach in entering the Second World War. Rather than keeping neutrality, Roosevelt made clear who the allies of the United States were and put large amounts of money into the wartime efforts. Roosevelt allied with Churchill and the British forces, in addition to the Dutch and the Australians. At the beginning of 1942, nearly 26 countries came together to form the United Nations; together these countries formed an opposition against the Nazi reign of Germany and Japan.

Through the development of the United Nations, in addition to Roosevelt's response to the Pearl Harbor attack and rallying a sense of patriotism among the American people, Roosevelt found himself faced with very few challengers for the Democratic nomination in the 1944 election. Changing his running mate to Harry S. Truman, Roosevelt defeated Thomas Dewey in the presidential election, winning again both the popular vote and the general election with comfortable margins. Interestingly, the fourth consecutive presidential election was arguably easier for Roosevelt than winning his third. Perhaps, this is because since he had already broken tradition and became president a third time, that the American people and other governmental and political figures were less hesitant to allow him to do it again.

It is thought that the American people saw Roosevelt as a symbol of progress and of the overall improvement of the United States. As he was able to bring the United States out of the Great Depression, wait until it was absolutely necessary to bring the Americans into the Second World War, in addition to making great strides with the allied countries to the United States, the American people believed that it would be him, Roosevelt, to help bring them out of the Second World War and any potential economic repercussions that were to follow. As a result, Franklin Delano Roosevelt and Harry S. Truman took office in 1944. Unfortunately for Roosevelt, he would not see many years of his fourth term.

## A Decline in Health

For many years in his presidency, the health of Franklin Roosevelt declined dramatically, though it was always being hidden from the American people when his health began to affect his physical appearance. Already being stricken with polio and suffering from complications of this illness, Roosevelt was already bound to a wheelchair by the time his third presidential term came around. As a result, it is suggested that he did not want to give the American people any more reason to view him as weak. However, in the early 1940s, Roosevelt began to look quite older than his age, thin, and frail. Of course, many American people ignored the physical appearance of their president as his mental faculties were clearly still strong.

However, by 1944, it was obvious that Roosevelt was quite sick. Not long after he turned 62, he was found to have high blood pressure, a coronary artery disease, and atherosclerosis: a medical condition where plaque builds up in the arteries and results in lesions both on the arteries and the external body.

Unfortunately, Franklin D. Roosevelt was unable to see the end of his labors as he passed away on the 12th of April 1945, less than a month before the war would end.

## Political Legacy

As you can see, the Roosevelt administration had their work cut out for them when they entered into the office of the president of the United States. This, however, helped Roosevelt be continuously elected term after term as he based his campaign platforms on what was the highest focus and concern of the American public at the time. For example, his first term was focused on relieving, reforming, and recovering from the Great Depression and the results of the First World War.

Then as the Second World War became more of a concern for the United States, Roosevelt campaigned on the promise that he had the interest of the American public in mind rather than simply showing the power and pedigree of the United States Army and Navy. Then when the entrance of the war seemed imminent, after the attack on Pearl Harbor, Roosevelt took charge and led his country confidently and fully into the Second World War. While still being hesitant and worried about what the Second World War would mean for the years to follow for the United States, Roosevelt paid close attention to the choices made by his predecessor Woodrow Wilson in the First World War. In an attempt to counteract and avoid the same mistakes, Roosevelt, in fact, consciously made the opposite decision that Wilson had years previously.

As a result, not only did the 4 terms of the Franklin D. Roosevelt's administration help to bring the United States out of the Great Depression and through the Second World War, but he also set an economic structure and different fail-safes that in the end allowed the United States to thrive after the Second World War and to avoid another economic downfall.

In the end, Roosevelt is seen as one of the most effective and productive presidents in the history of the United States.

\* \* \*

*"When you reach the end of your rope, tie a knot in it and hang on." —Franklin D. Roosevelt*

# Chapter Five: Life Beyond the White House

*"We must especially beware of that small group of selfish men who would clip the wings of the American Eagle in order to feather their own nests." —Franklin D. Roosevelt*

Of course, for any president of the United States, his life is not just the presidency. As we have seen in the earlier chapters, Roosevelt had a childhood and early life that contained, in its own right, an eventful and influential set of experiences. That being said, once Roosevelt was of age to begin his higher years of education, and subsequently as he was able to begin his career, it is clear that he was always aimed towards politics. After all, with such success in law school and his early entrance into the political arena, in addition to his natural charm and ties to a past president, it is hard to see or conceive of FDR becoming anything other than the Commander in Chief of the United States.

However, this does not mean that there were not moments in his life and tenure as President that were not significant in the total span of his life. Allow us to indulge in some of these moments and relationships here.

## Eleanor Roosevelt

Eleanor Roosevelt played a large role in the life and career of her husband in more ways than one. First was that she was the mother of her and Franklin's six children. To most women, both in the early 1900s and in the present day, being a mother to Anna (1906), James (1907), Franklin (1909) who unfortunately passed as an infant, Elliott (1910), Franklin (1914), and her youngest Jon (1916), would be enough to take up her time, giving little to no time to accomplish much else other than being a loving mother and homemaker. However, while she had been noted as being a good and loving mother, this lifestyle was not enough for Eleanor. Rather, she involved herself in politics more so than any other first lady, and arguably more than any woman before her time.

Her coming-out party, as it were, was the role and responsibility of maintaining her husband's credibility and good name within the Democratic Party while he was recovering from polio. Eleanor Roosevelt developed strong public speaking skills and was taken under the wing of Democratic participants of the House. From this moment on, Eleanor Roosevelt remained in the public and political eye alongside her husband throughout the rest of his political career. In fact, many political analysts credit Eleanor Roosevelt with taking the initial steps to making her husband the president of the United States. After all, if it hadn't been for her, his name would have faded from the minds of the Democratic Party during his political leave and absence.

Eleanor Roosevelt was born with the name Anna Eleanor Roosevelt, on October 11th, 1884. Niece of former President Theodore Roosevelt, Eleanor did not necessarily have an easy childhood. She experienced and suffered through the passing of both of her parents and one of her brothers before she was 16 years old. However, in the midst of this suffering, Eleanor Roosevelt was determined to continue her education and not simply be the stereotypical woman of the 19th and 20th centuries.

Eleanor Roosevelt has always been seen as a respected and well-brought-up woman despite her childhood suffering. However, in some circles, she was seen as controversial as she was quite outspoken compared to the first ladies that came before her. She would hold press conferences and contribute to magazine columns monthly, in addition to hosting radio shows and speaking at national conventions for political parties. Eleanor's high regard was also due to the fact that she mirrored many of her husband's favorable attributes. For example, Franklin D. Roosevelt was known for being quite direct and straightforward with his opinions on certain political matters. Eleanor, on the other hand, while she did not always agree with many of her husband's decisions or opinions exemplified the ability to support her husband while rationally refuting his claims. As such, she was seen as an intelligent woman who presented herself in a way that gave other women the confidence to do so. After her husband's passing, she had a political life of her own. She was the first delegate of the United Nations and served as the chair of the United Nations Commission on human rights. Furthermore, she headed the presidential commission on the status of women and administration under the John F. Kennedy presidency.

It was the same qualities that led her to have her own successful career in politics that allowed her to help and support her husband Franklin while he was recovering from polio. As mentioned previously, it was Eleanor's responsibility to keep her husband's name in the mouths of significant members of the Democratic Party in order to ensure, or at least try to ensure, that his paralytic illness would not limit his own political aspirations.

In the end, Eleanor Roosevelt was, and to this day, is seen as one of the most esteemed women not only in the United States but in the world as a whole. As such, it is nearly impossible to talk about Franklin Delano Roosevelt without mentioning his wife, Eleanor.


## Roosevelt and The Other Woman

Just as we cannot talk about Franklin Delano Roosevelt without making specific mention of his wife Eleanor Roosevelt, we cannot make mention of how poised Eleanor Roosevelt was, without making mention of her husband's philandering.

Lucy Page Mercer, born on the 26th of April 1891 in Washington DC, Is perhaps best known for her alleged affair with Franklin Delano Roosevelt. Having other family members being closely tied with Theodore Roosevelt, Mercer already had some sort of linkage to the Roosevelt family. However, it was in 1914 that Eleanor Roosevelt hired Mercer to become her own social secretary. Apparently, the affair between the president and Lucy Mercer began two years after this.

As the story goes, Eleanor and her children were vacationing while Franklin needed to stay behind in Washington. It was during these times that Eleanor was not in the country that Franklin and Mercer became close. They became even closer during the First World War when Franklin Roosevelt was the Assistant Secretary to the Navy and Mercer was assigned to work within his office.

The affair was simply rumors as many and witnessed Lucy and Franklin spending time alone together. However, the affair became, arguably, official when a relative of the Roosevelt family, namely Alice Roosevelt Longworth, encouraged the two to get together, inviting them to parties she was hosting. Through interviews, it can be drawn that Alice had a slight disdain for her cousin Eleanor, leading her to feel bad for Franklin and therefore encouraging him to have a good time with Mercer.

It was during their alleged affair throughout the First World War that Eleanor found a stack of romantic letters and correspondence between her husband and Lucy Mercer in his suitcase. As a response, Eleanor offered her husband a divorce. However, it was Franklin's mother who pushed him back to his wife Eleanor.

While both were willing to divorce and only didn't do so due to his mother's urging, the question left standing is whether or not Eleanor and Roosevelt truly loved each other. Based on a variety of interviews of their family members, in addition to some political specialists, the consensus is that while they still most likely loved and admired each other, the romantic and intimate love was no longer within the relationship. Rather, their marriage was more of a political and platonic truth and support system between the two individuals where Franklin used Eleanor's charm and cunning to help advance him in his political world, while Eleanor used Franklin's high status and eventual presidency to further her own means and goals of political and social influence.

Of course, as history tells us, the affair between Mercer and Franklin Roosevelt was not completely over. The two still kept in close contact with each other throughout the 1920s; even while Franklin and Eleanor had confirmed their marriage and Lucy herself had married another man. The correspondence made between Roosevelt and Lucy was done in secret; however, they were seen and noticed by some individuals including Franklin Roosevelt's secretary. As such, their secret correspondence did not stay secret for very long. In fact, the correspondence became so intense that Franklin enlisted the help of his daughter Anna, during his presidency, to arrange for secret meetings between Lucy and himself.

The controversy of the affair reached a deep end when it was found out by both Eleanor Roosevelt and the public that Franklin Roosevelt was in fact with Lucy Mercer at the time of his death.

### The Death of Franklin Delano Roosevelt

Franklin Delano Roosevelt, the 32nd president of the United States, passed away on the 12th of April 1945, at 63 years of age. At the time of his death, it is said that Franklin Roosevelt was sitting for a portrait to be painted of him. Throughout the process of the portrait being painted, Roosevelt made a comment saying that he had a terrible and terrific headache.

Quite shortly after this comment, he is said to have become unconscious, and hunched and slumped into his chair. As a result, the president's cardiologist, who happened to be there at the time due to Roosevelt's declining health in general, brought the president into the bathroom. Based on the symptoms and of Roosevelt's other health issues, Dr. Howard Bruenn diagnosed the medical mystery as an intracerebral hemorrhage. That is a brain bleed that takes place within the brain tissue. In other words, it is a type of stroke that is life-threatening, usually caused by the brain being deprived of oxygen and of its own blood supply. In modern times we now understand intracerebral hemorrhage, also known as ICH, to be brought on by hypertension.

Officially, Franklin Delano Roosevelt passed at 3:35 p.m. on an April afternoon. It was the next morning that Roosevelt's body was placed in a coffin and brought back to Washington; this is because Roosevelt was in Warm Springs, Georgia at the time of his death.

While the death of the 32nd president of the United States shocked the citizens of the country and the rest of the world, it was a somewhat controversial death for two reasons. The first was that Roosevelt's overall physical health, specifically the fact that it had been declining greatly over the last few years, was kept a secret from the American public. Only those individuals close to him know of the health issues he had been suffering. This false image of a healthy president was perpetuated by the fact that medical professionals and those individuals close to him claimed that the health of the president was nothing to be worried about. The other reason why the death of FDR was controversial, is the company he was keeping while he passed. Of course, he had a select few close advisors with him, including an on-staff cardiologist and doctor close to him, in addition to the painter herself, Elizabeth Shoumatoff. However, one individual who was only listed later as being present was Franklin Roosevelt's long-time love affair and mistress, Lucy Mercer. After experiencing the death of the president, she quickly left the cottage within which they were staying to avoid their secret escaping; of course, this didn't stop the news getting out eventually.

Although there are some controversies related to the death of Franklin Delano Roosevelt, it was still considered perhaps one of the most tragic deaths as he was such a highly revered and beloved leader of the United States. The painting that was begun on the day of his death was never finished and can be seen in its unfinished state at a retreat for Roosevelt named The Little White House in Warm Springs Georgia. However, following the death of her subject, Shoumatoff did finish a painted portrait of Franklin D Roosevelt that was almost identical to the one she had begun.

On account of the fact that President Franklin Delano Roosevelt was President for so long, four terms to be exact, in addition to the fact that his entire life was based in politics and helping to pull the United States out of the devastation of the First World War, help repair the Great Depression, and help to successfully get them through the Second World War, there was arguably little to no time for Franklin Roosevelt to develop any sort of life outside of his political achievements and aspirations, whether it be while he was president or in the years of being a minor political figure beforehand.

As such, most of his life beyond the presidency has to do with his wife, Eleanor Roosevelt, and his affair with Lucy Mercer.

* * *

*"We are a nation of many nationalities, many races, many religious - bound together by a single unity, the unity of freedom and equality. Whoever seeks to set one nationality against another, seeks to degrade all nationalities." —Franklin D. Roosevelt*

# Chapter Six: The Legacy of Franklin D. Roosevelt

*"Human kindness has never weakened the stamina or softened the fiber of free people. A nation does not have to be cruel to be tough." —Franklin D. Roosevelt*

With such success as the President of the United States, it is not difficult to understand the magnitude of the legacy Franklin D. Roosevelt left behind for both his family and his country.

The 32nd president of the United States was seen as one who was not only confident of the potential of his country but also honest and direct with his political message and movements. Throughout his presidency, Franklin Delano Roosevelt performed and shared what were known as fireside chats with the population of the United States. At times, he did this weekly, however, usually they were done sporadically. In these chats he would talk to the American people directly over the radio. It is within these fireside chats that he spoke with his American constituency and shared with them his political opinions, his aspirations and goals for the country, in addition to some rationale as to why he chose to follow certain political avenues over others.

As a result, he lessened the divide between the American people and their leader. Before the presidency of FDR, there was an unreachable and unattainable image of the president of the United States as he, theoretically and symbolically, sat above and overlooked the population of the United States. The only connection and direct communication he would have with the citizens of his country would be through the laws which he implemented and the policies and the laws which were passed down for his citizens to follow. In short, before the presidency of Franklin D Roosevelt, the citizens of the United States had very little, if any, understanding and knowledge of what transpired and went on behind the closed doors of the White House. An American political legend states that Roosevelt noticed a group of correspondents outside of his White House one day, standing in the pouring rain, waiting to communicate with the rest of the population what was going on, and trying to get some sort of a source for their story. As the legend goes, Roosevelt invited them into the White House to speak with them directly. That's when the presidential press corps was born. Whether this legend is true or not, many individuals believe it to be true.

It was also this transparency in his presidential methods that changed the role of the president from being an implementer of law and policy to an active partaker in the drafting of legislation and policy. As a result, Roosevelt then created a need for a larger group of advisers to work with the president in his day-to-day proceedings of the United States. This forever changed the form and shape of the White House and presidential advisers. In fact, the 1939 bill named the Executive Reorganization Bill allowed for this official change and structure to be carried through to the succeeding presidencies.

Honesty was not the only legacy that Roosevelt left behind. In fact, what is most impressive is that he is the only president to date that served more than two terms. From the time of George Washington and the creation of the United States as an independent country, it was an unwritten rule that the president was to step down from his role and allow other political party representatives to fight, debate, and challenge each other, and for one to be elected to the presidential house. This unwritten rule was widely accepted for over a century as it avoided the possibility of one individual gaining so much power over the country that it would mirror the monarchy of the country from which the United States gained its independence. Moreover, it allowed for an ever-changing and ever-improving economy, as it allowed for different ideals to be presented and pushed through Congress in order to continuously improve the country.

Of course, this all changed when Franklin Delano Roosevelt took office. Year after year, term after term the citizens and populations of the United States were never shaken from their confidence and allegiance to their president. As a result, he was elected to the role and office of the president of the United States for four consecutive terms. Although it worked out quite well for

Roosevelt and for the country of the United States, it was due to this four-term presidency that the 22nd amendment to the Constitution of the United States was added. In 1947, and ratified on the 27th of February in 1951, the 22nd Amendment placed official limitations of how many times an individual can be elected president and for how many terms. Specifically, that any one person can only be elected president for a total of two terms. Whether it be they are elected as president for two terms that are consecutive or two terms that have been spaced out over time, the limitation of being in office is for two periods of four years each.

Another part of the legacy that Franklin D Roosevelt left behind is that he was a president that changed the way presidents viewed the position itself, and the importance of the position in the eyes of the American public. Specifically, he changed the way that presidents dealt with the issues that arose and erupted during their tenure as president. For example, he did not necessarily deal with each challenge as its own individual issue. Rather, he looked at each issue as a way of connecting it back to the larger story of the United States and how he could use each problem to create success within the country both economically and otherwise.

For example, he did not deal with the issues that came up in the Great Depression with short-term solutions. Rather he took his time and developed a plan and deal that would allow for the

United States to have financial and economic security for many years to come. Similarly, he did not deal with the Second World War as its own issue, as he did not enter into the war right away. This was because he was concerned about the long-term effects that entering into a war would have on his country. Of course, after December of 1941 and the bombing of Pearl Harbor, his mind changed as his country was now being directly affected by the war.

This innovative way of conducting politics laid out the foundation for growth, security, and stability that the United States became known for, for many years to follow. Specifically, it laid the groundwork for what is now known as the Greatest Generation.

Roosevelt famously made mention to his Democratic party partners that the Democrats would not be able to take power in the United States until the Republicans brought the country into an ultimate state of despair and economic downfall. Of course, this comment was made by the to-be president in the 1920s, and as of course history has shown us the Great Depression followed in the 1930s. It is perhaps due to this comment that the citizens of the United States believed he was able to counteract the effects of the depression and shorten the amount of time that it would be lasting in the United States. After all, he did foresee such a catastrophic state of despair happening.

In his attempt to help the United States get through the Great Depression, he not only focused on those individuals who were let go or released from their jobs, but he also made sure to help those who could not work otherwise. For example: those who were too old, were ineligible due to their race or gender, or who could otherwise not work due to injury or malady. Again, showing his innovative politics for looking at each individual challenge as an opportunity to improve the greater picture. Of course, the New Deal did not fix everything, nor did it completely ease the stress of the Great Depression. However, it was the significant strides of economic improvement that instilled in the American public the confidence that it was Franklin Delano Roosevelt who would be able to lead them through the impending stress and conflict of the war happening overseas.

As mentioned previously, Roosevelt did not enter the war right away. Rather, he sent aid when able to while keeping his attention on his own country. Yet it was when Roosevelt decided to enter into the war that more confidence was placed in him by the United States citizens. This is because he entered the war not with the intention of simple retaliation or revenge for the Pearl Harbor bombing, but rather with the intention of showing the power of the United States. As a result, the influence that the United States had on the Second World War for the Allies helped to establish the United States with the reputation as the superpower that they are now known as.

While Roosevelt left his successors with the Soviet Union to worry about, he did leave those presidents to follow him with the tools, the governmental structure, and the political philosophy to be able to handle any other world issue that may arise.

When it comes to the legacy of the 32nd President Franklin Delano Roosevelt, he is largely compared to having an affinity with Abraham Lincoln. This is because both of these Presidents had similar political philosophies. Neither of them enjoyed or saw the reasons for war. However, when the time came to show their military strength, neither of them did so right away.

Secondly, both have the tendency to view the individual challenges that erupted during their presidency as parts of the larger picture and story of their country. Therefore, when it came to fixing or dissolving an issue, they always tried to fit the solution to their problem with another. Moreover, they were concerned with the years that would follow their presidency and the events that would happen in the United States after they had ended their leadership. Both presidents set into place legislative policies and acts that were intended to help improve the country, not only during their own presidency but for many years to come; perhaps in anticipation of the possible challenges the world would face. It is due to this political philosophy that Lincoln and Roosevelt alike are seen as being perhaps some of the most productive presidents during United States history because the acts and legislation created during their presidencies have lasted in the United States. Lastly, Roosevelt is often compared to Abraham Lincoln due to his transparent and direct nature and communication he had with the people of the United States. By communicating directly with the citizens of his country, President Franklin D Roosevelt was able to instill in his country a sense of confidence and relatability that many presidents that preceded Roosevelt, and many that succeeded him as well, lacked.

Ultimately, his actions during his presidency have led Franklin Delano Roosevelt to be regarded with perhaps some of the highest respect, appreciation, and regard of all presidents in history.

* * *

*"The liberty of a democracy is not safe if the people tolerate the growth of private power to a point where it becomes stronger than the democratic state by a group, or any controlling private power." —Franklin D. Roosevelt*

# Final Words

*"People acting together as a group can accomplish things which no individual acting alone could ever hope to bring about." —Franklin D. Roosevelt*

Of course, the presidency of Franklin Delano Roosevelt was not without its controversy, nor was it necessarily perfect. After all, there was the large controversy of his continuous affair with Lucy Mercer, his more of a friendship-like marriage with his wife, and Eleanor's outspoken and unconventional ways of presenting herself as a first lady that erupted during the Roosevelt presidency. Moreover, many economic specialists, in hindsight, have made the conclusions that Roosevelt's New Deal, although bringing about major improvements for the country, was not perfect, and Roosevelt's presidential challenger Herbert Hoover most likely could have had similar results if he were president during the Depression. It is perhaps the fact that Roosevelt was not perfect in his presidency that made him one of the more relatable presidents to his citizens.

No matter how you measure the accomplishments of a man, it is hard to discredit or disrespect a man who was able to overcome physical challenges in addition to some of the hardest and most challenging times of United States history.

There are numerous moments in the life and presidential run of Franklin Delano Roosevelt that make him one of the more memorable and influential presidents of the United States. Whether you hold in high regard the fact that he ruled one of the greatest nations from a wheelchair; or the fact that had a helping hand in leading and guiding the United States through two of the hardest parts of their history; or the fact that he remains to be the only president to serve four terms; or, lastly, that fact that he was influenced by his rambunctious cousin who once also held the title of president yet was able to make the role his own, FDR remains one of the most highly thought of presidents in the history of the United States.

In fact, surveys done in the United States since the 1940s have asked the citizens and population of the country to rank their most favorable, most productive, and overall best-performing president. It is interesting to note that Franklin D Roosevelt is almost always ranked within the top three; Usually, he's ranked third just behind George Washington and Abraham Lincoln. A placement that any president would be proud to hold.

With so many accomplishments on his punch card, it is hard for anyone to choose which one is the most important and most influential. What's more, with many of his historical moments still having ripple effects in the world today, one thing is for certain, FDR will not be forgotten in his role as president for quite some time to come.

* * *

*"The test of our progress is not whether we add more to the abundance of those who have much, it is whether we provide enough for those who have little." —Franklin D. Roosevelt*

# Timeline and Summary of Franklin D. Roosevelt.

❖ **1882**

➤ Franklin Delano Roosevelt was born on the 30th of January in 1882, to James and Sara Delano Roosevelt.

❖ **1900**

➤ Franklin attends Harvard University in Massachusetts; it was here where he was largely influenced by his cousin, Theodore Roosevelt.

❖ **1905**

➤ Franklin falls in love with Eleanor Roosevelt: Theodore Roosevelt's niece, making these two distant cousins. Despite this, they were married on March 17th, 1905.

❖ **1907**

➤ Roosevelt graduated from law school at Columbia University Law School and began a career in law at a top Law firm in New York at the time.

➤

## ❖ 1910-1913

➢ Roosevelt is convinced to run for a seat in the New York State Senate.

➢ In these same years, he was given the title and honor of being appointed Assistant Secretary of the United States Navy.

## ❖ 1920

➢ Roosevelt is chosen to be the vice-presidential candidate to run with James M. Cox against the Republican ticket: Warren G Harding and Calvin Coolidge. They lost the election.

## ❖ 1921

➢ Franklin D. Roosevelt suffered from polio in the summer of 1921. This illness leads to the eventual loss of his ability to use his legs.

## ❖ 1928

➢ Franklin D. Roosevelt runs and wins his election to become governor of New York.

## ❖ 1929-1932

➢ A time of great economic struggle, the Great Depression, proved to be a time of overall struggle and simultaneous creative political thinking for the United States.

## ❖ 1932

➢ Franklin D. Roosevelt is elected President of the United States. He tried to focus on bringing his country out of the depression.

## ❖ 1933

➢ On the 4th of March 1933, Franklin D. Roosevelt was inaugurated as the 32nd president of the United States.

## ❖ 1933-1936

➢ The United States experiences the positive consequences of the New Deal, however, only in part. As millions of individuals living in the country are still finding it hard to keep and hold jobs, Roosevelt, along with Congress, passed the Second New Deal.

## ❖ 1939-1940

➢ The Second World War begins in Europe. However, Roosevelt states that The United States will stay neutral and not enter the war yet. As such, he is re-elected for his third term as Commander in Chief.

## ❖ 1941

➢ Japan begins its assault and attack on Pearl Harbor in Hawaii. Roosevelt, as a response, implores Congress to declare war on Japan as retaliation, ultimately leading to the United States' entrance into the Second World War.

## ❖ 1944-1945

➢ Roosevelt was elected for his fourth term as president of the United States. During this term he is said to have met with Winston Churchill and Joseph Stalin to devise a plan to end the War.

## ❖ 1945

➢ After suffering from a cerebral hemorrhage while in Georgia, Franklin D. Roosevelt passed away. It was only a few months before the end of World War II.

# References

AZ Quotes. (n.d.). *400 QUOTES BY FRANKLIN D. ROOSEVELT [PAGE - 2]: A-Z Quotes.* https://www.azquotes.com/author/12604-Franklin_D_Roosevelt?p=2.

Content Time. (n.d.). *The Legacy of F.D.R.* Time. http://content.time.com/time/specials/packages/0,28757,1906802,00.html.

FDRlibrary. (n.d.). Franklin D. Roosevelt Presidential Library and Museum. http://www.fdrlibrary.marist.edu/archives/resources/timeline.html.

First Ladies. (n.d.). *First Lady Biography: Eleanor Roosevelt.* Eleanor Roosevelt Biography :: National First Ladies' Library. http://www.firstladies.org/biographies/firstladies.aspx?biography=33.

*Franklin D. Roosevelt's Presidency.* FDR Presidential Library & Museum. (n.d.). https://www.fdrlibrary.org/fdr-presidency.

Leuchtenburg, W. E. (2018, July 24). *Franklin D. Roosevelt: Impact and Legacy.* Miller Center. https://millercenter.org/president/fdroosevelt/impact-and-legacy.

Leuchtenburg, W. E. (2018, July 24). *Franklin D. Roosevelt: Life Before the Presidency*. Miller Center. https://millercenter.org/president/fdroosevelt/life-before-the-presidency.

Library of Congress. (n.d.). *President Franklin Delano Roosevelt and the New Deal : Great Depression and World War II, 1929-1945 : U.S. History Primary Source Timeline : Classroom Materials at the Library of Congress : Library of Congress*. The Library of Congress. https://www.loc.gov/classroom-materials/united-states-history-primary-source-timeline/great-depression-and-world-war-ii-1929-1945/franklin-delano-roosevelt-and-the-new-deal/.

The United States Government. (2021, January 15). *Franklin D. Roosevelt*. The White House. https://www.whitehouse.gov/about-the-white-house/presidents/franklin-d-roosevelt/.